BUILDING THE BEAR
A MID-MAJOR FUNDRAISING STORY

BRIAN GERRITY

SABBATH & BARON
BOOKS

SABBATH & BARON
BOOKS

© 2017 by Brian Gerrity

All rights reserved. No part of this publication may be reproduced in any form without written permission from Sabbath & Baron. sabbathandbaron.com

ISBN: 978-0-692-99227-2

Book Design/Graphics by Jordon Bruner
Cover Art by Lisa Cherry
Editing by Ciaran Cullen and Rachel Gerrity

DEDICATED TO RICK BOYAGES
MY FRIEND AND MY MENTOR

TABLE OF CONTENTS

1 | INTRODUCTION
3 | CULTURE
5 | WHY DO PEOPLE GIVE
7 | SET PRIORITIES
9 | GOALS
13 | YEARLY CYCLE
15 | PROGRAMMING

    17 | BEAR PLUS
    20 | 400 FUND
    22 | LETTERMEN'S CLUB

24 | SPECIAL EVENTS
27 | MAJOR GIFTS
32 | STEWARDSHIP
34 | MARKETING
36 | CONCLUSION

INTRODUCTION

Between 2012 and 2016, the Mercer Athletic Department experienced an explosion of growth in almost every area. During that span, Mercer Athletics won 13 conference regular season/tournament titles, set attendance records, changed conference affiliation, revived a FCS football program after a 72 year hiatus, and achieved at record levels in the classroom. This is the story of how the Mercer Athletic Foundation grew from a sleepy annual fund to a dynamic fundraising arm - funding the success of a mid-major Division I institution.

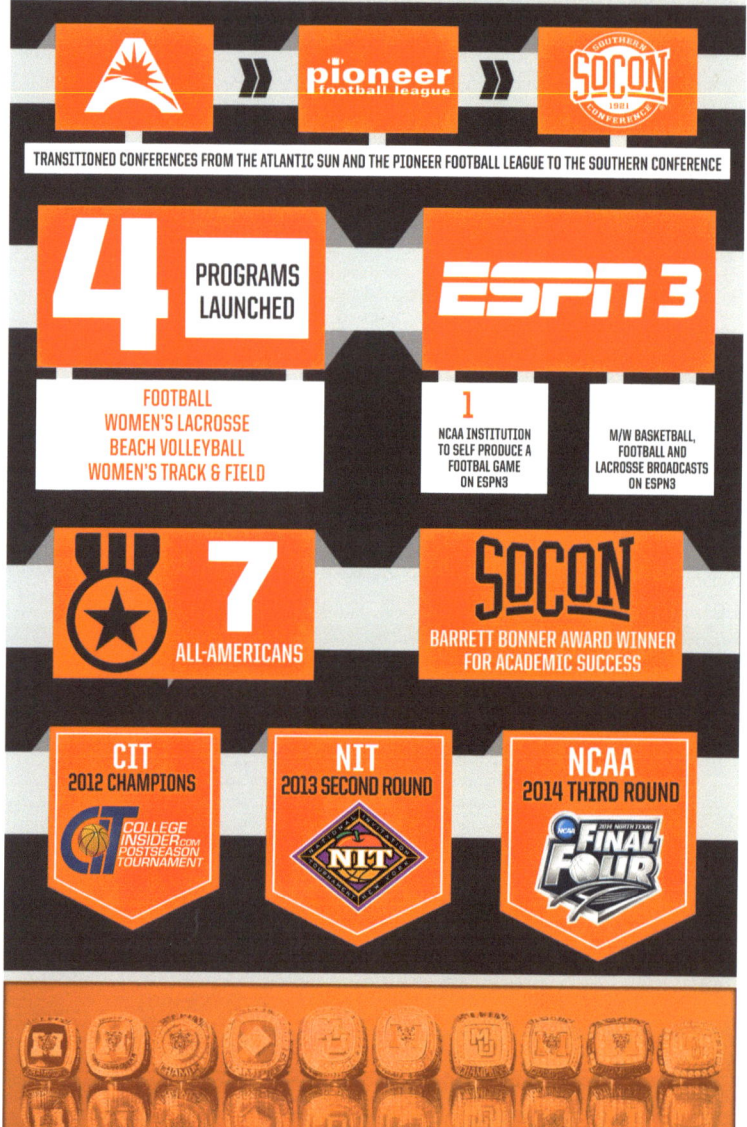

> "I'll go anywhere as long as it's forward."
>
> **David Livingstone**

CULTURE

The twenty year span before 2012 saw Mercer capture 10 regular season or tournament conference titles. **Between 2012 and 2016 Mercer has won 13 titles in seven sports.**

LEAGUE TITLES

Sport	Titles
BASEBALL	🏆🏆🏆🏆
MEN'S BASKETBALL	🏆🏆🏆
MEN'S SOCCER	🏆🏆
WOMEN'S BASKETBALL	🏆
MEN'S GOLF	🏆
MEN'S LACROSSE	🏆
WOMEN'S SOCCER	🏆

What changed? Why the sudden success? When Jim Cole assumed the role of Mercer's athletic director in 2010, his first major task was shifting the culture of the department. Cole's philosophy and goals for the culture of the department echoed those of Mercer's President Bill Underwood, an aggressive, competitive, smart, and passionate leader who wanted to excel both athletically and academically. The energy and enthusiasm injected into Mercer's department by Cole, along with several key mantras laid the foundation for wide-ranging success.

MANTRAS

TAKE RISKS
- INVEST IN BILLBOARDS ANNOUNCING FOOTBALL'S SIGNING DAY CLASS IN TIMES SQUARE
- JUMP TO THE SOUTHERN CONFERENCE AND SCHOLARSHIP FOOTBALL AFTER ONE SEASON OF COMPETITION

BE CREATIVE
- SHIFT TO ESPN3 AHEAD OF SOCON PEERS
- PEP RALLIES/PARADES THROUGH ASHEVILLE, NC AT THE SOCON TOURNAMENT

BE OPEN TO CHANGE
- ENHANCE DIGITAL/SOCIAL MEDIA TO STAY AHEAD OF THE SOCON
- ELIMINATE LONG GAME PREVIEWS AND RECAPS AND SHIFT TO HYBRID BULLET STYLE RELEASES

MAKE GAME DAY SPECIAL
- FIREWORKS, BEAR WALK, INFLATABLE VILLAGES, MASCOTS ON MOTORCYCLES, REPELLING IN FROM THE RAFTERS, PRE-GAME CAR SHOWS, DELIVERING THE GAME BALL BY PARACHUTE, GIVEAWAYS, INTRO HYPE VIDEOS, AUTOGRAPH SIGNINGS, TEAMS CIRCLING THE COURT POST GAME TO INTERACT WITH FANS.

These mantras have fueled a shift in the culture at Mercer. Staff members are not afraid to chase a new idea, push a new initiative, or start a new program. Creativity is valued and no idea is out of the realm of possibility. Mercer's culture has allowed for dynamic and creative growth simply by letting young, talented, and smart staff members think outside the box.

The culture of the Athletic Foundation echoes that of the Athletic Department and has allowed for growth in annual giving, programming, major gifts, and overall enthusiasm. Once the cultural stage was set, the Foundation was ready to grow.

> Don't tell me where your priorities are. Show me where you spend your money and I'll tell you where they are.
>
> James W. Frick

WHY DO PEOPLE GIVE

The motivations behind giving are usually simple. Donors are either philanthropic or motivated by benefits. When designing programming, it is critically important to develop programming that plays to both interests.

Between the time the Athletic Foundation was established until 2012, no major benefits existed. The standard benefits chart did exist, but no branded programming to inspire donors wanting an enhanced game day experience to give was available. Each year, donors would support the Foundation because they loved the school, wanted to support their alma mater, or wanted a tax deduction.

The installation of programming to capture the casual fan and establish a baseline of transactional giving was the top priority before the start of football in 2013. A program was needed with strong benefits that not only encouraged new donors but rewarded those who had been giving to Mercer for years.

With strong programming in place, casual fans would become donors to take advantage of benefits. The existing traditional donors would continue to give for philanthropic reasons. This layered approach to fundraising, capturing both transactional and philanthropic gifts, would provide the framework for massive gains in giving totals.

BENEFITS "GIVE TO GET"

- TRANSACTIONAL IN NATURE
- DOES NOT ALWAYS TRANSCEND WINS AND LOSSES
- GAME DAY EXPERIENCE TRUMPS "SUPPORTING"
- MOTIVATED BY SEATS/PARKING/BENEFITS

PHILANTHROPY "LOVE"

- TRANSCENDS WINS AND LOSSES
- ACCOMPANIED BY INSTITUTIONAL PRIDE
- INTEREST IN IMPACTING STUDENT-ATHLETES AND LOCAL COMMUNITY
- MOTIVATED BY HELPING THE INSTITUTION

A balance between both philanthropic and transactional giving is important to maximize revenue. Options for both fans and loyal alums must be available. Is a donor "less" important because they care more about their seat location than their impact on the institution? Is a donor "better" because they care deeply about the institution? To be successful, both ends of the donor spectrum must be satisfied - those giving for benefits and those giving out of the goodness of their hearts.

> Good things happen when you get your priorities straight.
>
> Scott Caan

SET PRIORITIES

Before establishing programming, overarching organizational questions needed to be answered. What is the priority? Unrestricted giving? Program specific restricted gifts? Establishing endowments? The process of determining priorities needed to be carried out before any programming could take off. The question, "where is the Foundation going" had to be answered before starting down the path of soliciting gifts.

After meetings with senior administration, senior advancement staff, and the athletic director, it was determined that unrestricted giving was the most critical need. Establishing a roadmap for the next four years was the key - starting with unrestricted giving as the focus, moving towards major gifts, and finally shifting focus towards endowment.

The most basic decision, the unrestricted gift focus, was made after carefully analyzing the pros and cons between restricted and unrestricted gifts. The key reason unrestricted giving was decided as the focus was the impact unrestricted gifts could have on the ENTIRE department and the DECISION MAKERS in charge of spending the money raised.

By focusing on unrestricted gifts, Mercer's Athletic Director has the ability to use the money raised on predetermined and strategic initiatives. If money was wrapped up in sport specific accounts, it would limit his ability to take on current year small to medium projects. In other words, the power to decide how money was spent stayed with the administration who had a larger and clearer view of the "big picture."

RESTRICTED GIFTS

- EARMARKS GIFTS FOR SPECIFIC PROGRAM OR FUND
- LIMITS SPENDING POWER AND ALLOCATION FOR ATHLETIC ADMINISTRATION
- BUDGET REPLACEMENT VS. BUDGET ENHANCEMENT
  (SOME SCHOOLS USE PROGRAM SPECIFIC GIFTS TO REPLACE BUDGET, SOME USE IT TO ENHANCE BUDGET)
- CON: LIMITS ABILITY TO TAKE ON SMALL TO MEDIUM SINGLE YEAR PROJECTS
- CON: RICH V. POOR PROGRAMS (SOME PROGRAMS WOULD RAISE MORE THAN OTHERS)

UNRESTRICTED GIFTS

- NO SPECIFIC DESIGNATION FOR GIFTS
- GIVES ATHLETIC ADMINISTRATION POWER TO USE FUNDS FOR DEPARTMENT NEEDS
- ABILITY TO BALANCE SPENDING BETWEEN PROGRAMS
- ABILITY TO TAKE ON SMALL TO MEDIUM SINGLE YEAR PROJECTS
- CON: SOME PERCEPTION THAT ALL MONEY IS USED FOR REVENUE SPORTS
- CON: ATHLETIC ADMINISTRATION'S USE OF MONEY MAY NOT BE POPULAR WITH STAFF/COACHES

Additionally, money in "one pot" allowed for visible and noticeable changes within the department. For example, during the 2014-2015 academic year the Athletic Foundation covered the cost of championship rings for two fall sports (roughly $30,000) and purchased an inflatable bear that is used at basketball, football and lacrosse games ($16,000). The roughly $46,000 to purchase those items came from the Athletic Foundation general account - decided upon by the athletic director. If the Foundation focus was restricted giving, the ring money would have been split, $15,000 per program, from women's and men's soccer. The inflatable bear money would have been split equally between the programs that benefit from its use. Those totals would be astronomical for a single program at a mid-major like Mercer to cover, and the priority for spending by the individual programs may not include something to enhance the game day experience like an inflatable bear.

One of the core job responsibilities of any sitting athletic director is effective budget management - why take the power away from the person charged with managing the budget by restricting dollars to an individual program?

 Setting goals is the first step in turning the invisible into the visible.

Tony Robbins

GOALS

Goal setting was the next logical step after determining unrestricted giving as the priority for the Foundation annual fund. The MAF goals needed to be broad, follow a path, and lead to expansion and growth in dollars raised, staffing, programming, and focus areas. With football on the horizon and the Foundation in its infancy, the goals began as simple and straight forward and moved towards more complex initiatives.

YEAR 1

In 2012, the only Athletic Foundation materials on file were a simple benefits chart, a season ticket flyer for the start of football in 2013, and a database of past donors. The motivation for giving was purely philanthropic. The roster of Foundation donors were nearly 95% alumni. A shift in demographics needed to take place to fund the upcoming football related expenses. The first action taken during 2012 was developing and installing a preferred seating and parking program for football. Simultaneously, an emphasis was placed on getting out on the road, soliciting alums, community members, and ticket holders to meet the University goal for the Foundation. Until 2012, the Foundation never came within 50% of the University goal.

YEAR 1 GOALS
- ENGAGE DONORS
- DEVELOP/INSTALL FOOTBALL PROGRAMMING
- MEET UNIVERSITY ANNUAL FUND GOAL

YEAR 2

2013 was the first year of competition for the football program. The preferred seating and parking program (Bear Plus) was in full effect, and the top priority was selling the program and educating donors about the benefits, renewal timelines, and policies. In year one, the Foundation met and exceeded the University goal - for year two the goal was still focused on growing the annual fund and renewing members. There was a dramatic and dynamic shift in the demographics of the Foundation during the growth. The installation of the Bear Plus program led to a shift in membership. The 95% alumni membership dropped to roughly 50% alumni and 50% community. This shift showed the popularity of the program for the casual fan and the interest in supporting football by the Middle Georgia Community.

YEAR 2 GOALS
- GROW FOOTBALL PROGRAMMING (BEAR PLUS)
- EDUCATE DONORS
- GROW ANNUAL FUND

YEAR 3

By year three the Bear Plus program was enjoying great success. Membership numbers were still growing and the community had continued to support the program. Two potential problems, however, were identified throughout the first two years of the program.

Giving for benefits, or transactional giving, could be "fleeting." Ticket holders who take part in the program that have no deep interest or ties in the institution may not renew if the football team does not perform at a high level or if their interests change.

Donors are directed towards the two main levels of Bear Plus. Potential dollars were being missed from donors who had the capacity to give more but were taking part in the program.

The solution to address these potential problems was the 400 Fund. This named, current use scholarship program created a giving level above Bear Plus with a unique set of benefits. Rather than giving to "get" something, donors involved in the program are paired with a student-athlete. This program does not depend on wins and losses, does not tie into a game day benefit, and instead shifts the donor intent away from simple benefits and back towards traditional philanthropy. Donors in this program feel good about the impact they are making on a specific athlete. In other words, this program shifts donors away from transactional giving and "humanizes" their gift. They are making a difference.

With two major programs now in place, it was important to be able to educate our donors in an efficient and effective way. The classic and typical benefits chart would no longer suffice and mailing brochures was both costly and inefficient. The need for a Foundation specific microsite was evident and the design and launch of supportmaf.com was a critical win to support the growth the Foundation was experiencing. Additionally, more staffing was needed. Through lobbying to Advancement, Athletics, and the University CFO, the Athletic Foundation staffing pool was increased to handle the influx of donors, interest, gifts, and programming.

Along with more staffing came the ability to shift focus towards major gifts. During its first three years, Foundation growth was primarily focused on establishing the annual fund - the engine that drives the Foundation. With the annual fund clicking and moving in the right direction, coupled with three years of relationship building, the time to make major gift asks surfaced. The incredible influx of major gifts during years three and four were made possible through effective annual fund management and strong relationship and trust building as football returned to campus.

YEAR 3 GOALS
- DEVELOP/INSTALL HIGHER LEVEL PROGRAMMING (400 FUND)
- IMPROVE ONLINE FOOTPRINT/PROGRAMMING
- SHIFT FOCUS TO MAJOR GIFTS
- GROW ANNUAL FUND

YEAR 4

The strategy behind year four was simple. Steward donors who had started major gift commitments, grow the 400 Fund roster, and renew Bear Plus members. Year four was as much about maintaining relationships as it was about "selling." At this point, donors were comfortable with the calendar, renewal cycle, and annual fund events. Major gift donors were in year two of their commitments, and 400 Fund members had established good relationships with their designated student-athletes. Donors were being ushered up the annual fund ladder and seeing the fruits of their major gift commitments through the groundbreaking of a new baseball stadium, complete overhaul of the tennis facility, and major upgrades to the basketball arena.

The next step for the Foundation was enhancing endowment opportunities and discussing the long term future of the Foundation. To ensure financial stability for generations, endowment had become an attractive and straightforward solution. Additionally, endowment asks were made to a completely different subsection of Foundation members and alums. Endowment is about legacy, the future, and leaving a mark for generations to come. Endowment offerings spoke to a donor class that transcends current operational gifts. Focusing on endowment will be the single most important action the Foundation takes moving forward.

YEAR 4 GOALS
- STEWARD MAJOR GIFTS
- GROW HIGHER LEVEL PROGRAMMING (400 FUND)
- GROW ANNUAL FUND
- BEGIN FOCUS ON ENDOWMENT

> You take care of every day
> let the calendar take care of the year.

Ed Wynn

YEARLY CYCLE

Prior to 2012, the Athletic Foundation calendar was simple. The start of the fiscal year was July 1, end of the fiscal year was June 30, and two major solicitation mailings were carried out in the fall and spring. There was not programming tied to any specific sport or event, and no key prompts throughout the year to encourage giving other than calendar and fiscal year ends. By establishing programming tied to a sport (football), the need for a calendar of key dates was critical. The best example of this is the April 30 deadline for Bear Plus (preferred seating and parking program for football) renewals. Prior to the start of the Bear Plus program, April 30 was no different than February 10, June 1 or any other date. Due to the installation of programming and a calendar, April has become one of the biggest months for giving simply because of the renewal deadline.

The yearly annual fund calendar is as much for donors as it is for internal staff. Donors like to know what is on the horizon and plan accordingly. A strong calendar and clearly educating donors about key dates will lend to sustained annual fund success. People like to help, they like to make an impact, and the calendar shows them how to do so. Additionally, when special events happen - for example making the NCAA Tournament or student travel to a conference tournament - working to fund those initiatives can happen because the broader framework of the year is already in place. The calendar is a shifting and evolving document which allows for special circumstances but ensures accountability for basic operations.

The Athletic Foundation calendar today is dramatically different than the simple "fall and spring" mailing calendar of the past.

ANNUAL CALENDAR

JULY-SEP.
RECRUIT NEW BEAR PLUS MEMBERS

AUG.
WELCOME BACK DINNER/400 FUND DONOR DINNER W/ATHLETE

SEP.-NOV.
STEWARD DONORS/BASKETBALL PREP/ SPECIAL EVENTS (FOOTBALL)

NOV.
BEAR PLUS RENEWAL MAILING

NOV.
HOMECOMING/FALL MAF BOARD MEETING

NOV.-APR.
BEAR PLUS RENEWALS

MAR.
DONOR DRIVE CHALLENGE SPRING MAILING

MAR.
SOCON BASKETBALL TOURNAMENT

APR.
SEASON TICKET RENEWAL DEADLINE

APR.
SPRING MAF BOARD MEETING

MAY-JUNE
NEW BEAR PLUS

MAY-JUNE
END OF YEAR PUSH

JUNE
END OF YEAR MAILING

 Clarity trumps persuasion.

Flint McGlaughlin

PROGRAMMING

Three major prongs of programming are currently sponsored by the Athletic Foundation: Bear Plus, the preferred seating and parking program for football; 400 Fund, the named current use scholarship program; and Lettermen's Club, a lower level giving society for former student-athletes. When designing each program, it was important to be clear and simple with the end game of each. Want better parking? Join Bear Plus. Want to make an impact on a student-athlete? Join 400 Fund. Want to give back to your alma mater? Join Lettermen's Club. While the benefits range from dinners to parking to Facebook groups, the purpose is clear: support Mercer to provide a championship level experience for our student-athletes.

The branding and naming of each program was purposeful and important. A number of institutions offer benefits that are similar to Mercer - but the presentation of the benefits is how the Foundation is different. Some schools bury the same benefit in a larger chart. Others just list "required gifts" for different sections alongside a diagram of the stadium. That type of presentation lends to conversations between donors which include:

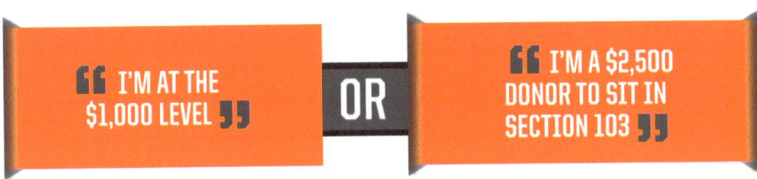

By branding the programs the following dialogue is created instead:

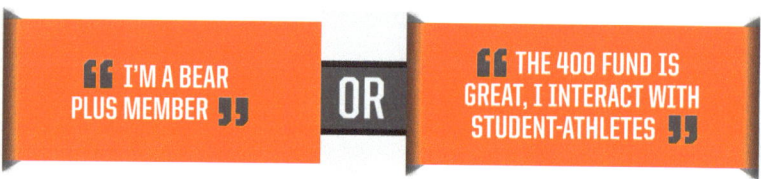

The terminology is not about a dollar amount - it is about being part of a program.

"I am a Lettermen's Club member" encourages curiosity about the program, leads to others visiting the Foundation page to learn more, and sounds special. "I give $100 a year to the Athletic Foundation" does not inspire or sound unique.

The branded programming at Mercer is similar to that of other institutions- make a gift and receive an upgraded experience. The key difference, however, is the way it is packaged.

BEAR PLUS

With the rebirth of Mercer Football set for fall of 2013, the 2012-13 fiscal year was critically important to capture the excitement surrounding the program within the Mercer alumni base and the community. A preferred seating and parking program needed to be installed, and during the summer of 2012 the Bear Plus program was developed.

WHAT IS BEAR PLUS?

THE BEAR PLUS PRIORITY SEATING AND PARKING PROGRAM IS DESIGNED TO ENHANCE THE GAME DAY EXPERIENCE BY PROVIDING OPTIMAL SEATING AND UPGRADED PARKING FOR THE MOST PASSIONATE MERCER FANS. ONLY UNRESTRICTED GIFTS QUALIFY FOR BEAR PLUS UPGRADES.

When creating the program, several key points were necessary for a successful launch:

1. The program needed to reward long time donors with high lifetime giving totals
2. The program needed to encourage new donors
3. Only unrestricted gifts qualify for Bear Plus membership
4. Do not require a gift for ALL season ticket purchases, just Bear Plus donors
5. Brand the program

With the five points listed above in mind, the Bear Plus design process was ready to begin. Five clear and distinct steps during the development process were followed:

STEP 1
Define the Bear Plus sections as the lower and upper bowl sections on either side of the 50 yard line (the best seats).

STEP 2
Determine seating priority. The following order was used to determine the seating priority:

1. Bear Plus membership (to qualify for center section seats)
2. Lifetime giving to Athletics
3. Lifetime giving to the University

The three tiers to determine seating priority allowed for long time donors and new donors to have the best seats. First, to qualify for the best four sections, donors needed to join Bear Plus. Once qualified for Bear Plus, lifetime giving became the separator. The largest Athletic Foundation lifetime giving got the first choice of seats. For "new" donors, the $2,500 level was given priority over the $1,000 level. Those with high lifetime giving were rewarded for their years of giving by getting first choice of seats, while new Bear Plus donors were leapfrogged over the rest of the season ticket holders into the best sections. The third tie-breaker was lifetime giving to the University - which was not necessary to use during initial seating because no two donors had the exact same lifetime giving.

STEP 3
Decide on membership levels by wrapping into overarching Foundation and University benefits:

1. MAF Level ($2,500) doubles with Athletic Foundation Board membership
2. Preferred Level ($1,000) doubles with President's Club membership (campus wide program for donors of $1,000 or more).

STEP 4
Differentiate membership levels through parking.

1. MAF Level membership includes NAMED parking spot adjacent to the stadium.
2. Preferred Level membership includes first come, first served parking in closest proximity to the stadium.

STEP 5
Develop a catchy, branded name for the program.

With Bear Plus the decided upon name, the levels agreed upon by University administration, priority for seating set, and the benefits clearly outlined, the "sales" process began. An influx of community members, alums, and friends of the program jumped at the opportunity to join. By pricing the Bear Plus experience far below a similar package at Georgia or Georgia Tech, Mercer differentiated itself within the market. Additionally, basketball parking was wrapped into the program - adding a tremendous amount of value to Bear Plus membership.

Bear Plus quickly became a common term within the Mercer community and the base of the Athletic Foundation was set for future growth.

400 FUND

By 2015, three years into Bear Plus, the program had become the standard of giving for the Athletic Foundation. Donors had either become "Bear Plus donors" or "non Bear Plus donors." The terminology for the Foundation had literally shifted and Bear Plus/Athletic Foundation had become interchangeable. On one hand, this was fantastic - the marketing of the program worked and the Mercer community had gotten behind a great program with powerful benefits. On the other hand, the program had limited some prospects to the published Bear Plus levels rather than giving based on their capacity. Additionally, the transactional nature of Bear Plus had led to some donors "giving for benefits" rather than giving to support the athletic program. The time had come to introduce new, higher level programming which shifted away from standard transactional giving and more towards philanthropic intent.

When designing the new program, the first question asked was about giving intent. When all of the perks, parking, tickets, facilities, and naming opportunities were boiled down, the most obvious reason for philanthropic giving was the student-athletes themselves. Everything revolved around supporting, nurturing, and helping the student-athletes mature into the best versions of themselves. Alums are quick to help student-athletes have a championship level experience. Community members made Mercer Athletics a point of community pride and wanted our student-athletes better served than our Southern Conference counterparts. At Mercer, like many institutions, actions are based on the needs of our student-athletes.

The name of the program, 400 Fund, refers to the headcount of the Mercer Athletics program - roughly 400 student-athletes. Additionally, this name came as a shock to a number of alums. The Mercer athletic department had grown dramatically over time - in the last decade adding football, men's and women's lacrosse, beach volleyball, and women's track & field. The department had nearly doubled during the last decade leading up to 2015 (with most of the growth since 2012).

HOW IT WORKS

STEP 1 — MAF WILL PAIR A DONOR FAMILY WITH A CURRENT STUDENT-ATHLETE.

STEP 2 — THE STUDENT-ATHLETE'S SCHOLARSHIP WILL BE A NAMED CURRENT USE SCHOLARSHIP FOR THE DURATION OF THE 3 YEAR COMMITMENT.

STEP 3 — EACH YEAR, THE ATHLETIC FOUNDATION WILL PROVIDE SPECIAL OPPORTUNITIES TO INTERACT WITH THE DESIGNATED STUDENT-ATHLETES.

The intent of the program, beyond raising needed current use funds, is to expose donors to student-athletes on a personal level. The program includes a three year commitment, not four. This is to give internal staff a full year to determine the best athletes for the program - those who are personable, serious, and intent on staying at Mercer rather than transferring. Program rules clearly state the department is charged with selecting the student for the donor. The reason is based on two factors - first, NCAA rules, and second, insurance that a donor is placed with an athlete who would mesh well in terms of personality, field of study, and future career aspirations. It was very important for Foundation staff to work with both compliance and donors to ensure all NCAA regulations were followed explicitly.

With over 30 donors taking part in the program in year one, 400 Fund has fast become an aspirational program for donors. Careful thought goes into unique donor gifts, preset interactions with the student-athletes, and cards/videos during holidays. 400 Fund donors are treated with an added level of care and the student-athletes selected for the program understand the importance of their relationship with the donor.

LETTERMEN'S CLUB

The 400 Fund program and the Bear Plus program both cater to donors at the $1,000 level and above. While both programs satisfy different populations- philanthropic intent with 400 Fund and game day enhancement with Bear Plus, a key demographic was missing. No programming existed specifically for former student-athletes. The thought behind the Lettermen's Club was to engage former student-athletes, help the overall University alumni giving percentage, bring alums back to campus through special events, and help the overall membership numbers for the Athletic Foundation.

Additionally, one key theme that was central to the development process was to provide easy access for young alums. By engaging student-athletes at graduation and instilling a culture of giving back early, down the road these same former student-athletes will be more apt to give at a higher level. In other words, the Lettermen's Club provides an avenue for young alums to be involved with the Athletic Foundation.

The benefits for this program were developed to encourage quality interaction.

WHO IS IT FOR?

FORMER STUDENT-ATHLETES, CHEERLEADERS, MANAGERS, TRAINERS AND COACHES.

1. A special keepsake for members after their first gift
2. Provide opportunities for members to come back to campus
3. Engage with the membership throughout the year

With those three elements in mind, the benefits were developed to encompass each. First, with input from several former student-athletes, a membership coin was developed. The coins fit perfectly in a trophy case, on a desk, or even could be used for a ball mark when golfing. The investment in quality coins in full color were an instant hit with former student-athletes. Next, a football game was selected for inviting Lettermen's Club members back to campus. The coin was used for the coin toss, members were invited on the field at halftime for recognition, and pregame all members were invited to the Athletic Director's tailgate. Lastly, and most important, was the development of the Lettermen's Club Facebook page. Each week the page was updated with "Member Monday," "Throwback Thursday," and other content to allow for constant and dynamic interaction with the membership. This is a closed group - only comprised of Lettermen's Club members. The Facebook page allowed for more quality interaction with alums than any other avenue the Athletic Foundation offered.

> Having an aim is the key to achieving your best.
>
> — Henry Kaiser

SPECIAL EVENTS

In addition to general programming, challenge style events have been a key element to successfully growing the annual fund. Each year the Foundation sponsors two special events - one called the Donor Drive Challenge and the other something new and unique to the current year. The purpose and aim of these events are two-fold. First is to increase participation. Second is to raise dollars for a specific initiative.

Donor Drive Challenge

Each spring, the Foundation sponsors a week long event to solicit donor participation for a specific initiative. The first, hosted in 2013, was geared towards raising the funds needed to purchase high definition cameras and other equipment to launch an ESPN3 studio on campus. The total cost of the equipment needed was $100,000. The goal was straight forward - raise $100,000 in one week and solicit as many gifts as possible. The rules for the challenge, which have remained the same each year, are as follows:

There are two goals for each Donor Drive Challenge - one is monetary and one is participation. Both goals shift according to need each year. The participation goal is between 200 and 300 gifts and the monetary goal is between $30,000 and $100,000.

If both goals are met, two sponsors "match" with a $30,000 gift.

All gifts must be received during the challenge week.

The challenge is set up to value small participation gifts as well as encourage larger gifts to help reach the monetary goal. The 2016 challenge added another twist - any donor of $1,000 or more towards the challenge was listed as a "Donor Drive All-Star" in the post event release. The donor who contributed the largest gift towards the challenge was named "Donor Drive MVP." For the 2016 challenge, an influx of $1,000+ gifts were received specifically to be named an All-Star.

The challenge is heavily marketed through the following outlets:
1. Splash page on athletic website
2. Full release on athletic website and local news outlets
3. Hard mailing to over 8,000 households
4. Social media posts throughout the week of the challenge
5. Email blasts to past donors/alums

Between 2013 and 2016, the challenge raised nearly $400,000 towards ESPN3 equipment; a fund designated to purchase tablets for student-athletes; sponsorship of the year-end student-athlete banquet; and to establish a enhancement fund for use by Mercer's athletic administration.

Other Challenge Events

Other challenge events are not scheduled but are rather reactionary. The use of additional challenge events are either to capitalize on a time-sensitive event or to defray an unexpected expense.

Defray cost: After the men's basketball team defeated Florida Gulf Coast University to advance to the 2014 NCAA Basketball Tournament, Mercer's President decided to sponsor hotel rooms and a bus trip for any students who wanted to attend. This trip was WILDLY popular and for Mercer's first game 5 bus loads of students made the trip to the Tournament. After an upset win over Duke, 7 bus loads of students made the trip for the next round against Tennessee. The bus and hotel bill was astronomical and the Athletic Foundation was charged with soliciting funds to cover the cost. This cost was not expected but through a quick mini-challenge campaign, the trips were covered.

Capitalize on an event: Kyle Lewis, Mercer's centerfielder, was named the 2016 consensus national player of the year and projected as one of the top draft picks in the MLB Draft. Leading up to the draft, the Athletic Foundation launched a "guess the draft position" challenge revolving around Lewis. The total dollar amount raised was not significant, but the challenge publicized Lewis' success, allowed donors to interact with the Foundation in a fun and easy way, and added a good deal of new donors to the Foundation membership.

Challenge style events are a perfect opportunity to raise significant dollars and push for new members in a unique and different way. The challenge gives the perfect "excuse" to make a cold call, network with current donors, and bring the Foundation to the front page of the athletic website.

> "Donor loyalty is not about the donor being loyal to you, it is about you being loyal to the donor."
>
> — Harvey McKinnon

MAJOR GIFTS

Between 2015 and 2016, the Athletic Foundation has solicited and received multiple seven figure gifts, over ten six figure gifts, and a host of five figure gifts. The gifts have been designated for a wide variety of items spanning from facilities, to program enhancement, to naming opportunities, to endowments. The influx of major gifts during this span are a result of several key elements - from relationship building, to attractive initiatives, to new facilities. The methodology, planning, and solicitation strategies developed before an ask is made is as important as the ask itself.

Trust

Developing a level of trust with a donor and major gift prospect is critical to success. Trust relates to every aspect of the major gift process - relationship building, the ask itself, stewardship, and use of resources once gifts begin to come in. Trust becomes visible before, during, and after the ask. Does the donor trust in the direction of the Athletic Foundation? Does the donor trust their resources will be used effectively and in a timely manner? Does the donor trust the gift officer making the ask? Does the donor trust the vision of the Athletic Department? All of those questions dictate the comfort level in giving a major gift. Without trust, aligned vision, and the department moving ahead with projects after a gift is solicited, a major gift program will fail.

Planning

A clear, outlined, dynamic plan for revenue and facility enhancement is critical to the success of a major gift program. Does the department need endowment dollars? Is a facility in dire need of a renovation? Is the annual fund performing and hitting target numbers? Each of those questions are covered in a master plan. At Mercer, the priorities are drafted in a single document which outlines the coming five years. The document details revenue projections and rank orders projects based on priority. This document is critical on the fundraising end - not only to understand the priorities of the department but to build a plan and have "ammo" when talking with donors. Also, the blueprint sets hard revenue goals for each project which assists in yearly planning.

Strategy

The solicitation strategy is different with each and every ask. Some follow the traditional script - develop a relationship over 18-24 months, research capacity/interest, make an appropriate ask. Others require presenting to a board of directors or partners at a business - one chance to present then wait for a positive vote. Still others require thinking on the spot - a donor offers an amount and asks how it could best be used. Each avenue poses different thought processes and requires a different skill set, but each requires a deep and intimate knowledge of the direction of the department, vision for the future, and immediate needs. During the 2015 and 2016 calendar years, each strategy was employed at Mercer to solicit and secure major gifts.

Seven-Figure Naming Commitment for Football Stadium
The Five Star Automotive commitment to name the football stadium followed the traditional major gift timeline. Between 2013 and 2015, the co-owner of the auto group was engaged by the Athletic Foundation in a number of ways. First was election as President of the Athletic Foundation board. In this capacity, he was involved with every aspect of the Foundation. He saw the numbers, developed trust, and was heavily involved with identifying the departmental needs. The ask was made during halftime of a basketball game on the sidewalk outside the arena. The ask was straightforward, honest, and short. The ask secured the interest and the "YES"- the details were then worked out over the course of a month.

FIVE STAR STADIUM

ORTHOGEORGIA PARK

Seven-Figure Naming Commitment for New Baseball Stadium
The OrthoGeorgia baseball facility naming ask followed a completely different script when compared to Five Star. This ask was made in a presentation to the partners of OrthoGeorgia, the largest Orthopedic group in Middle Georgia. The presentation was thorough and included renderings of the facility, a mock ESPN3 broadcast opening using the OrthoGeorgia Park intro, and a question and answer segment. A tremendous amount of research and planning went into this ask, including an analysis of the dollars spent with OrthoGeorgia each year by the Athletic Department. After a successful vote to proceed with the naming, multiple drafts of a naming agreement were traded between Mercer and the group before the final draft was agreed upon.

Six-Figure Commitment for Tennis Facility Renovations

While this gift started with relationship building similar to the Five Star process, this gift was completely donor directed. The donor had a clear love of tennis and wanted to make a gift to impact the program. After making this interest clear, it was the job of the Athletic Department and Athletic Foundation to develop a renovation plan and timeline to present to the donor. One key element to this ask was a limited timeline - the donor wanted the project to be completed in a 3 month span leading up to a professional tennis tournament hosted on Mercer's campus. Trust was a major factor on both ends - trust the project would be completed on time and trust that a multi-year commitment would be honored. The private tennis gift fully funded a new scoreboard for the tennis facility ($70,000) and landscape/hardscape renovations ($179,000).

PRIVATE TENNIS GIFT

PRIVATE UNRESTRICTED GIFT

Six-Figure Commitment for Unrestricted Use

This gift was the most unusual and unexpected gift secured by the Athletic Foundation. The donors were the grandparents of a football player and had high capacity and an initial meeting to talk about the Athletic Foundation was set. Within five minutes of the meeting start, the donor broke conversation and said "I will give you a $100,000 check today - what is the best use for it?" While unexpected, without understanding the overarching needs of the department this would be a difficult question to answer. Instead, without hesitation, the answer was unrestricted support. Allow the Athletic Director to use the funds to enhance the department in the current year.

Purpose/Timely Use

Both purpose and use go hand in hand in major gift fundraising. The purpose (what the money will be used for) and timely use (in other words get the project done in a timely manner) are critically important when interacting with a major gift donor. Before a donor says "yes" to supporting a project they must understand the scope and purpose of the project. Questions like "why are we building this" or "how will this impact student-athletes" need to be addressed before moving forward. Additionally, while it sounds simple, sometimes a project can run long or not even be started. Clear communication is imperative to keep the donor happy and up to date on progress.

A perfect example is OrthoGeorgia Park. While the lead gift and several additional major gifts were solicited and secured in 2015, the architectural work took nearly a year to complete. It is important to understand the timeline and have a strong relationship with the donor to ensure everyone is on the same page. The staff and partners at OrthoGeorgia understood the need for a new stadium and the impact it would have on recruiting and fan experience. On the timeline end, the OrthoGeorgia doctors understood that work couldn't be done during the season and that architectural renderings and construction negotiations take time. Many times donors assume that a gift is made and a project starts immediately. The honest and upfront communication with OrthoGeorgia throughout the planning stages kept them happy and engaged with the project leading up to the groundbreaking.

> Transparency, honesty, kindness, good stewardship, even humor, work in businesses at all times.
>
> John Gerzema

STEWARDSHIP

Stewardship is a word commonly used in the development world but many times is misunderstood. To most people, stewardship is saying thank you or sending a thank you note. Effective stewardship involves much more and requires an intimate knowledge of the donor base. Stewardship is not a once a year act - it is a constant throughout the course of a relationship.

Keys to successfully steward a donor

Write thank you notes. At Mercer, throughout the course of the year a hand written note is sent to each and every donor. Gift level does not matter on this front - a $25 donor receives a note the same as a $1,000,000 donor.

Answer the phone. When a donor calls, answer. Sometimes it is just to talk, other times the donor needs something. The Athletic Foundation is the front door to the athletic department for most donors. The Foundation staff may be the only people the donor knows in the department.

Follow through. When a donor needs something, get it done. While a request may sound small or insignificant, to the donor it is important. Each act of following through and producing for a donor earns trust and positive feelings towards the institution. Don't let small items fall through the cracks.

Understand the big picture. Daily conversations with donors need to be positive. Donors may give to secure football benefits but do they know about the great things the soccer program is doing? By understanding the larger picture of the department and being on the "inside," the Foundation can provide donors with information that can't be found by looking at the athletic website or attending a basketball game. Have talking points across all programs (including general university items) and be ready to answer questions about each sport.

Know your donors. Some donors will ask the same questions every time they call. Some donors don't care about wins and losses and want to know about academics and community involvement. Others would rather talk about women's golf than football. Some are Hall of Fame members and others are community members. Knowing donors on a personal and deep level lead to better relationships. Think of donors as partners, not dollar signs - **GET TO KNOW THEM**.

Only ask once. Each fiscal year donors are only solicited once. It is important to know when donors give (some give each year in December, others in June) and to make an appropriate and timely ask. Donors understand they will be asked for money - it is the Foundation's job to raise the dollars needed to operate the athletic department. What they don't want is to be asked for money during every interaction with the Foundation. By only asking once each year, the rest of the year can be used to develop trust and a deeper relationship. Donors come to expect the ask each year and don't feel like they are being used for their support.

Stewardship takes many different forms from going to lunch with a donor to providing tickets on the road to just calling to talk. Strong stewardship is the biggest key to building a successful donor program.

> **People don't buy what you do, they buy why you do it.**
>
> — Simon Sinek

MARKETING

Prior to 2012, marketing the athletic foundation was never made a priority. The donor base supported because they loved the school - not for benefits or a larger impact. When marketing the Foundation, several key elements needed to be addressed to shift from simple philanthropic support to being a part of something bigger.

Website overhaul. The development of supportmaf.com added instant legitimacy and a central hub for Athletic Foundation information and programming. The website also separated Mercer from peer institutions and made a statement about the importance of athletic giving. When designing the website, it was important to tell a story. The long scroll format encompasses the mission statement, projects, Foundation leadership, includes photos of athletes and fans, and touches on the successful growth in giving. The key positioning of student-athlete photos is a constant reminder about the core mission of the athletic department - give student-athletes a championship level experience.

Branding programs. As discussed earlier, the branding of Foundation programming has been critical to building membership and lends to a feeling of being part of something bigger. Instead of just being a donor, members are part of the program.

Game day culture. Game day is the best and most efficient way to touch a large number of donors simultaneously. When designing the game day layout - everything from parking to entrance points were discussed with the atmosphere in mind. Bear Plus donors not only needed the "best" lots, but attractive green space to tailgate. Bear Plus was not just a program with a parking pass - it became a program with access to the best tailgating and networking. From tent cities to RV parking to the Bear Walk, game day has been set-up to create a culture of excitement, enthusiasm, and positive energy.

Shift Foundation Board membership. In 2012, the Athletic Foundation board consisted of a core group of loyal, longtime supporters. The first goal in relation to the board was to shift board membership into a who's who of Middle Georgia. The goal was to ensure the board is about more than just the Athletic Foundation - it is about networking with the power players in the region. Instead of stuffy and boring meetings, strong interaction with the members was delivered through guest speakers as well as question-and-answer sessions with University leadership.

Rings. The championship ring is the most striking and powerful symbol of success within athletics. The athletic department made a clear policy that both regular season and conference tournament championships would earn rings. The adage "success breeds success" relates perfectly to the Foundation's use of championship rings in almost every publication. People want to be associated with winning programs - the use of rings in materials show that success in a bold way.

Creative and unique donor gifts. Each year thought and effort is put into the decision about donor gifts. In 2012, gifts consisted of cotton t-shirts or Mercer pens. The goal was to develop gifts that would be keepsakes, used, put on a donor desk, or talked about. Between 2013-2016 the Foundation has given custom glass cutting boards, massive detailed foam fingers, gear, coins, football helmets, logoed golf balls, and framed art. When visiting Foundation member offices, donor gifts are usually on display and always talked about. Using the gifts as marketing pieces in the community rather than giveaways has enhanced the legitimacy of the Foundation.

DO EVERYTHING WITH THE STUDENT-ATHLETE IN MIND. This has been the most important marketing tool employed by the Athletic Foundation. Specific student-athlete stories are told. Projects are brought back to the impact they will make on the student-athletes. Game day enhancements are sold as impacting the student-athlete experience. Every conversation revolves around the student-athletes and that constant reminder helps when soliciting gifts. This is not for Mercer…it is for the student-athletes.

Marketing is traditionally thought of in the framework of game day experience, in-game promotions, sponsorship activation, and ad buys. Effective marketing of the fundraising arm is just as important - through visible items like a website or brochure as well as by word of mouth by donors and community members.

CONCLUSION

The Mercer Athletic Foundation is still growing and changing at a rapid pace. The successes in fundraising between 2012 and 2016 have been a testament to strategic thinking, loyal alumni and friends, and the Middle Georgia community embracing Mercer Athletics. The strategic vision for the next five years will no doubt be different, creative, exciting, and filled with enthusiasm.

 It takes a lot of courage to show your dreams to someone else.

Erma Bombeck

www.ingramcontent.com/pod-product-compliance
Lightning Source LLC
Chambersburg PA
CBHW042053290426
44110CB00006B/176